a thousand voices whispering

Arlene Angeles Biala

Sampaguita
Press

a thousand voices whispering
Published by Sampaguita Press
P.O. Box 731305
San Jose, CA 95127

www.SampaguitaPress.com

Cover art and design: Frances Mendoza

ISBN 978-1-965439-10-4

This publication is made possible by funding provided in part by the Montalvo Arts Center, SVCreates, Local Color, and other generous contributions from our readers. Our heartfelt thanks for your support.

Praise for
a thousand voices whispering

"Arlene Biala's *a thousand voices whispering* is a living archive of memory, grief, and resilience. It is an intimate chorus of voices carried across oceans and generations. Through poetry that moves like both prayer and testimony, Biala transforms family histories of migration, trauma, and survival into sanctuaries of connection and courage. Immediately personal and collective, this collection insists on remembering, even when remembering hurts, and shows how poetry can document, heal, and sustain. It is a vital contribution to the literature of diaspora and survival, a book that will linger like a song refusing silence."
—**Tshaka Campbell**, Santa Clara County Poet Laureate Emeritus

"*a thousand voices whispering* is a reckoning with the trauma of the past on the poet's family. History haunts us in the generational body and soul of who we are as a people. Arlene weaves the oral interviews from her elders' painful memories of hunger and war, depression and suicides, as if in a ritual cleansing and exorcism to release the grip and shame of colonial oppression on her own psyche as well as those of future descendants. The power of memory to reclaim control over one's narrative strikes at the goal of Settler Colonialism to silence and erase its victims' cultural identity and voice. Arlene Biala's voice in this respect, becomes a thousand voices echoing."
—**Genny Lim**, San Francisco Poet Laureate, Performer, Playwright, Educator, Activist

"Experiencing *a thousand voices whispering* is having poems help you ask permission to enter a forest or bring you oceanside to listen to stories made of water and salt, in an offering of intimacy with a family's fullness of curses and blessing. Arlene Biala breathes so much life into these poems because they center on the people she loves, especially those who silently suffered while the world continued to move on. *a thousand voices whispering* is an altar holding atangs (food offerings). It is a place of confessions and prayers, and a gallery of faces whose spirits still shape the lives of the living."
—**Lorenz Mazon Dumuk**, Author of *Held*

"Arlene Biala's new work moves us through Filipino Voices in the Diaspora — their inscapes of trauma and endurance. A groundbreaker completed during her fellowship at Montalvo Arts Center where I had the fortune of writing a poetry book on Darfur, Africa — *Senegal Taxi. a thousand voices whispering* is a priceless and loving tribute to her pamilya."
—**Juan Felipe Herrera**, Poet Laureate of the United States 2015-2017
Robert Frost Medal, Poetry Society of America, NYC, 2024
Ruth Lily Prize, Poetry Foundation, Chicago, 2023

"Arlene Biala masters the art of poetic storytelling in her most recent collection, conjuring women who have since joined the ancestors or will be gracing their presence soon in the Other Realm. One of the great responsibilities of the poet is to give voice to the voiceless, where Biala takes up the arduous task of being mouthpiece for women of her lineage who had been silenced for much too long. In the juxtaposition of matrilineal perspectives across generations, Biala shows us what has been forgiven, what remains mired in guilt, and where deep examinations across generations serve as promises to continue healing forward."
—**Elsa Valmidiano**, Author of *We Are No Longer Babaylan* and *The Beginning of Leaving*

"Arlene Biala's work is the remedy our communities need. Her poems move like prayers, gentle yet powerful medicine for our minds, hearts, and spirits. She reminds us that the pain we carry is not only our own but part of a lineage, passed down through generations. Yet, within that inheritance, she shows us we also carry the medicine to heal. Her poetry is a reminder that healing ourselves is an act of love and resistance. It is how we make space for abundance, for joy, and for the future generations who will inherit the worlds we are creating today."
—**Yosimar Reyes**, Santa Clara County Poet Laureate, Writer, Activist, Performing Artist

Arlene Biala's *a thousand voices whispering* takes polyvocality through interviews with her matrilineal family, where interviewing is holding aunties' hands through their memories and silences. Biala's poetry takes on the rigorous, emotional challenges of oral history, and weaves narratives that redefines what Filipino languages do not have a word for: mental health. Biala's poetry sings the songs and secrets of her beloveds to understand herself. We need these stories.
—**Janice Lobo Sapigao**, Santa Clara County Poet Laureate Emeritus
Author of *Microchips for Millions* and *Like a Solid to a Shadow*

for my mother, my rock
maria gloria angeles biala

and

my angeles family
from mapandan to the bay

to re-grow
a tongue, pull it from beneath silt at the bottom of the sea.
if it is knotted, frayed, tangled, you can take up my voice.

~ Art 25: Art in the 25th Century,
Future Ancestors

Contents

12   **invoking you**
     13   before we begin
     14   call
     15   response
     16   family photograph
     18   trigger warning

20   **kindred**
     21   bitter
     22   mom says
     23   nanay says
     25   when i ask mom to recall the albularyo she visited in san diego, she says
     26   nanay bening. orasyon. anting-anting
     28   crowned queen at 86

32   **sisters - part one**
     33   tips for interviewing the sisters
     34   before the interview begins i say
     35   when interviewing the aunties
     37   rookie.   my first group interview
     41   *agayla bii ya*

42   **time of war**
     44   fire ants
     45   when the japanese soldiers arrive
     46   to hide from the soldiers at night
     47   sari sari
     48   being exposed
     49   american soldiers

50   **sisters - part two**
     51   auntie charing says
     52   *i have the receipts*, mom says
     53   auntie lumie says
     57   naani   later
     58   we don't talk about it being a problem until it is

60   **to want to be a saint**
        62   hay(na)ku: **to want to be a saint**

76   **brothers**
        77   1. i dream us, uncle e
        80   dear uncle joe,
        82   uncle rafael says

85   **descendants of angels**
        86   cousin jennifer (naty's daughter)
        89   niece frances (naty's granddaughter)
        92   niece bea (charing's granddaughter)

94   **ascending**
        96   devotion
        97   ate gigi,
        100   dear niece b,
        102   dear nephew,
        104   every unexpected

106   **the bending of waves**
        109   hay(na)ku   maria gloria (mom)
        110   *so anyway* . . .
        112   mom confesses
        113   anak na lassi
        114   mirror   salming
        118   mom
        120   talking about war
        122   mother daughter
        124   anting-anting.

126   dear readers, a word

129   notes & acknowledgments
130   translation index
134   list of mental health resources
136   acknowledgements

a thousand voices whispering

invoking you

before we begin

drop your shoulders

have you slept?
have you eaten?
have you moved your body?

name three things you can see right now
now three things you can hear
and three things you can touch

does your chest feel heavy?
are you aware of your breathing?
find a sign that triggers calm

like the smell of your dog's corn chip paws
or the mourning dove's five-note mantra
greeting you after a full night's insomnia

can you whisper, then scream
the name of someone you love?
close your eyes. wait.

inhale	*two*	*three*	*four*
hold	*two*	*three*	*four*
exhale	*two*	*three*	*four*
rest	*two*	*three*	*four*

repeat

call

bari bari

may i come in

may i do no harm
in asking my ancestors
to breathe with me
in grief and laughter alike

will you protect me

bari bari   bari bari
i close my eyes
call for your grace
listen for your breathing
to silence the voices in my head

i feel your palms pressed
together in prayer
when you finish,
i take your right hand,
lift it to my forehead

mano po, bless me
with your burdens,
with your forgotten joy
may all beings be free
from suffering

i call for your forgiveness
when the remembering
splits open wounds
you thought were sealed

i call for peace among sisters
who say too much and still
not enough, i call for voices
to erupt from the throats
of brothers who felt
no choice but to leave
abruptly, watching us
lost in their wake

response

one thousand voices
whispering
bari bari

wading
trembling
drifting

bari bari

we are still here

we miss you

we call your names

one thousand voices whispering

bari bari
walk up the hill
burn the sage before entering

bari bari
hang the family photographs
over the altar

bari bari
close my eyes and listen
for your voices

bari bari
bamba, jr, uncle emy, uncle joe
i can hear you

bari bari
will you sit with me awhile
so i can breathe

bari bari
we can laugh at the full moon
and call everyone home

family photograph

clockwise from top left

marie mercedes	mer	aunty merced	grandma mer
maria natividad	naty	aunty naty	grandma naty
maria iluminada	lumie	aunty lumie	grandma lumie
maria gloria	atsi glo	aunty gloria	grandma gloria
maria rosario	char/rosario	aunty charing	mamang
emmanuel	emy	uncle e	
joseph	joe	uncle joe	
felipe	tatay		tatay / lolo eping
rafael	raf	uncle raf	grandpa raf
benedicta	nanay		nanay / lola bening
maria beatriz	bett/beatriz	aunty betty	grandma bet

trigger warning

this book is ripe with triggers

bari bari   *tabi tabi po*
yes, go ahead and ask
the dwende for permission
to be disturbed, but

be careful what you ask for
ripple effects stalk you softly
attack when you least expect it
a weak pulse turns thunderous
hundreds of miles beyond
this shoreline you walk
this surf break you swim
how many days, months, years
it may take to reach you
submerged swell gathering force
on its way to you, triggered now
and barreling toward you,
no time to move out of the way

trigger warning: parenting.
somewhere we fail, fall easily
into autocorrect passed down
from our own. what the fuck.
we never asked for this.

my son and i share the same pills
to help us be still. when we panic
we have to remind each other
how to ride the waves when they hit.
how to stay present. the inhale, hold,
slow exhale of our breathing. tapping
the corners of our eyes, cheekbones,
jawline, clavicle, sternum. on loop.

listen. there is no answer to answer,
no guarantee these words will heal

you or help you resolve. hands tremble
while we brace for you.

glimmer warning: i want to say
that i love you beyond. forgive me
for exploring the layers of your tongue,
scraping surface to bleed memory.
please take more time
than you think you are allowed.
pause. look around.
take a deep breath and wail.

kindred

I forget how we approach writing and start writing what's missing.
I get lost and tell no one. I let the book sink until it's become
another form of emptiness. I'm more interested in its lack.

~ angel dominguez, *Black Lavender Milk*

tambal   remedy

bitter

i hated it so much.
the american soldiers took over our town during the end of the occupation.
they set up medical services at our elementary school. i was ten years old.

> *pluck bugayong leaves from the vine.*
> *rinse, mash, boil and strain*
> *to a pulp.*

they had a dentist check all of our teeth.
that's how i found out my tooth was rotting and infected.
that's how i found out what triggered my asthma.

> *force yourself (or let someone force you)*
> *to drink*
> *to bring up bile.*

but the bugayong gave me hives. the itching was unbearable.
i was always ironing towels and then would slap them on my body to get relief.

> *repeat three times*
> *a week. do this to get rid of asthma*
> *triggered by infected tooth.*

it didn't last long so i kept doing it.
maybe that's why nanay assigned me to the ironing of everybody's clothes
since i was always using it anyway.

mom says

they all thought i was a señorita
she's always inside, akin
stuck all day in my room
with the sad iron pressing clothes

        arawi   far away

anak na lassi, sangi ka
nanay would force my mouth
to swallow the bitter drink
tickle my throat with a chicken feather
to make me throw up the bile

my sisters said i would sleepwalk
in the garden and stop to look
at the moon with my eyes closed
they said i was the lucky one

because i got to leave first
honestly, i didn't want to go
but tatay said *go pack your things*
your husband needs you

i had a one-way ticket
i was 25 years old
14 weeks pregnant
never rode an airplane

        taynan   to journey

i wanted to go home
as soon as i stepped out
from the plane in san francisco
the wind slapped me

my face, my hands froze
the fog was swallowing me
i didn't even have a coat
i couldn't stop shaking

nanay says

of course, your mom was the señorita
because she was so sickly growing up
she had to stay inside just to breathe
only watch her sisters playing outside

      kapalaran   fate

her duty was to iron the clothes
sometimes i would catch her
sleepwalking through the garden
like she was looking for the moon

          bii   female

she was the lucky one. she left first
she didn't want to go but tatay told her
you better go, your husband needs you

      pikakasi, dasal prayer

she was pregnant when she left home
i was so scared because i didn't know
when i would see her again. my anak,
my first born. but what can i do.

I think this may be said of all memory:
A body is forgetful.

~ angel dominguez, *Black Lavender Milk*

**when i ask mom to recall the albularyo she visited in
san diego, she says**

it wasn't me who got cursed. it was nanay bening. many times. and also
aunty charing and aunty merced. aunty mer got extremely sick.

*but didn't you go to see the albularyo to see if your cancer diagnosis was
from a hex placed on you during your last visit home to mapandan?*

(breathe, two, three, four . . .)

oh, yeah. that's right.

uncle jess drove through the night because they told us he would see
me early in the morning. albularyo only see people on tuesdays and
fridays because that is when their power is stronger.

i remember sitting in the living room alone. he was in a separate room
but i could see him through the slits in the bamboo partition. he stayed
in the room while he asked me questions. how was i feeling. when did i
start coughing. was it getting worse quickly.

then i was quiet. his voice changed. i heard a voice emerge that
sounded like a young child, a boy maybe only five or six years old.
i couldn't fully understand what he was saying but i felt very calm
listening to his voice. later his assistant told me he said don't worry,
manang. it will pass. you are going to be okay.

this was before i got the news from the doctor that i had lymphoma.
remember, the doctor said i might have only three months to live?
thank god that albularyo was right.

nanay bening. orasyon. anting-anting

ay hija, i've been cursed many times

one time, I was only sixteen
my god, i had so much pain
my stomach was so bloated
i felt like i was dying

i went to the albularyo
after he examined me, he said
aye dios, someone put something inside
your stomach. you better drink this right now
and he gave me a plastic cup

my god, the taste was so sour it made me cry
i threw up everything in a big pool on the floor.
it took a long time, but then i felt okay.

that albularyo was so excited.
he screamed, *engkantos, engkantos!*
and his voice was so high-pitched
like an altar boy but he was already so old
maybe he was 70. i cried because i was scared

pero, i was okay after that.

panangasi'y diyos

mom and nanay. backyard celebration of mom's remission from non-hodgkins lymphoma

crowned queen at 86

hi, nanay. is it okay to talk now?

> *mmm. sige. gala dia*

did you secretly get married?

> *i didn't want my daughters to know. they don't approve.*

jimmy told me you said, "yes, i'm married" at the christmas party.

> *sssssssssshhhhhh*

but did you really get married? or you wanted to get married but didn't?

> (no answer)

i remember you holding a whole apple pie at the farmers market when i ran into you. i heard all your daughters screaming in my head, "nay! you can't eat that! too much sugar! susmaryosep, you're going to end up in the hospital again!"

> *i just smile at them and wave, haha*

i remember walking through your front door at plaza de las flores. your husband(?) vincent's body splayed on your living room floor. eyes, mouth open. dark red clotted sticky substance i still smell over thirty years later.

but i can't remember seeing the gun. i don't remember why he did it.

> *never mind. ang sakit na ulo.*

i'm sorry, nanay. here, drink some water.

- - - - - - - - - - - insert story - - - - - - - - - -
what happened when he proposed to her

Nanay Bening, crowned Her Majesty the Queen

(L to R): Naty, Charing, Nanay Bening, Gloria, Merced, Betty
Coronation ceremony

sisters
part one

tips for interviewing the sisters

1. ask mom to invite her sisters.

2. gather at aunty mer's house on sunday afternoon in november.

3. bring the garlic fried rice. the box of pinipig polvoron. extra AAA batteries.

4. greet everyone. sniff kiss. eat first. tsismis. listen while they joke about their crumbling bodies, rusty knees, pollen allergies, insomnia, blood pressure spikes.

5. stay ready to hit "record"

6. ask open-ended questions. let them lead.

7. breathe deeply to keep calm while they talk over each other.

8. pay close attention to the one who doesn't speak.

9. try not to let tsismis turn tsunami.

10. be prepared to stay years longer than you had planned.

before the interview begins i say

you don't need to share anything
that you are uncomfortable sharing

i will not publish anything i write
without letting you read it first

if you would rather be anonymous
just let me know. it's fine, really

if you are okay with me recording
our conversation, i will record

on this. if you want me to turn it
off, just let me know

i ask if they have ever felt
depression or anxiety

if they knew what it was
if they just tried to ignore it

it is only about three minutes
before aunty charing points

with her lips to tell me
turn that off now

a procedure that was supposed to be minor . . . ~ maria bolaños

when interviewing the aunties

i keep wandering through your homeland
trying to find mine. ducking under the cautionary
tape, *bari bari*, i hesitate, mumble
my apologies but i'm still trespassing
no idea if this trail is a loop or dead end
in a vertical drop off the precipice.
the more you know the less you know

how addictions work. craving
sweetness while devouring
your memories.

i confess i don't know where this is going
beyond intention to make way for your voices
i am not a documentarian. i am not a mind reader.
i wasn't really *there*. aside from seven generations.

i am none of the four attributes of god:

god is	omnipotent	all powerful
god is	omniscient	all knowing
god is	omnibenevolence	all loving
god is	omnipresence	all existing, all directions, all

here, and, nor, there. diaspora whispers
become wind gusts on whitecaps where
nobody in their right mind would want to be

please forgive me. my questions may disturb you.
feeble attempts to find a cure
without knowing the root causes. side effects

are often worse than what makes you sick.

last night i saw a wave. the first in a set
of monstrous breaks i wasn't ready for,
fury slamming me onto the reef
    i was gasping   spinning into the hold down
    praying to god   waiting to drown   in all
i opened my eyes and saw you.

rookie.   **my first group interview**

gloria: your aunty betty is our cnn. we call her the chronicle. she never came home when it was time for dinner. always the last one to arrive. because she's outside in the neighborhood all the time, *in the neighborhood they said this . . ., somebody has a new . . . oh my god i just heard tita pilar say that kuya ben was at . . .*and tatay would start laughing because nobody   could stay mad at her.

lumie: kuya hermie i mean your dad was supposed to court shirley, the enamorada but he chose your mom instead. he knew what to do. i mean, you better know to go greet tatay first if you're courting one of us. otherwise you're dead.

gloria: your aunty mer and aunty naty were the quiet ones. very sensitive. they were buddies, always hanging out together. they have their own secrets. they are closer to tatay because he understood them somehow. maybe because they were sensitive. naty used to just sit down in the corner and cry. maybe that's why she had that early ulcer. she didn't express herself.

mercedes: i was a tomboy. i'm always climbing the (coconut) trees, doing anything outside. i never tasted my mom's milk! we had a goat and that's my "mom", i drank her milk. we took the goat everywhere.

i know all the secrets of my brothers because i was the one who played with them, hang around them all the time. i'm the one who always begged tatay to leave them alone. i remember begging him because your uncle emy used to refuse to eat or talk. one time he wouldn't eat for a whole week. he really scared me.

lumie: i was 26 when i came here. oh, kiddo. i got a horrible story. i was ready to kill myself if your mom and dad didn't petition for me to come. i was really ready to end everything. your mom was lucky, she had already left. it was hell what happened to us there.

so anyway, do you remember when tatay beat up nanay? she was all bloodied, she had to be taken to the hospital. i was working in manila at that time. i got a telegram. anyway, sinting was our chaperone. she was always with us per tatay's orders.

oh, your aunty had back luck with her admirers. she had to elope.

charing: my husband didn't want to leave mapandan. we had our business and it was already doing good. we used to keep tons of money in the rice sacks. it wasn't atsi glo who petitioned me. nanay did.

gloria: i still have the receipts! i petitioned you first, not nanay. your name kind of slid out. you and your kids. we had to wait fifteen years for approval of that petition.

jennifer (naty's daughter): i remember mom screaming when she got the notice of approval in the mail. she almost gave up, thought we weren't meant to come over. then all four of us got approved at the same time. after that, it still took three years to come over.

gloria: every friday night we would sneak downstairs after nanay and tatay went to bed. we gathered in the living room around 1am to talk, eat, dance. not just us sisters, our brothers, too. neighbors and their tsismis wondering who were our noisy visitors so late at night. it was just us. nanay would get so mad because we would eat all the bananas and other snacks. she would wake us up at 6am, throw open the

curtains, notice the food was gone. she would yell at us *anak na lasi!*
you guys are like goats!

lumie: that guy, he had a half-brother who was with the daughter of
the aunt, what was her name again? the sister of my grandma (my
cousin jen and i look at each other totally confused.) uncle max!
maximo angeles. half-brother of tatay. remember rafael and ben, the
"mosquito net" children (you know, that's what we call the bastard kids
of tatay's half-brother) who died of syphilis. you don't remember? that's
from cha bibing. (conversation switches to pangasinan)

gloria: nanay used to boil bananas, ordered your auntie lumie and char
to go sell them around the neighborhood. she only made me do it one
time because when the neighbors would tell me they didn't have money
i would say just take them and pay later. when i got home nanay yelled
antoy gagawen? where's the money? and i said *they didn't have it, they'll
pay later*. she got furious with me.

she used to blame me because i was the oldest. me and my sisters
would be walking home from church, but the socialite sisters were
always behind, talking to people. that's how they are. nothing i could
do about that.

gloria: nanay was all about saving money. she made our clothes. she
would buy one bolt of fabric and make the same dress or shirt for all of
us. then, ok, haircut! and she would give us all the same bowl cut.

mercedes: the thing with tatay is that he was so strict. if you lie and
didn't pass it to the other one (you know, like make sure your stories
were the same) if he caught one of you, he would get everyone.
everyone got in trouble.

me: was tatay more strict than nanay?

mercedes: when he is mad, she starts in, too. it made it worse. she didn't protect us. instead of protecting us, she fuels the flame, aggravates it.

gloria: your aunty mer got married in 1965. then she got pregnant and had bernie in may 1966. your aunty naty had joey first, april. then charing with rocelyn. then came bernie, then you in june. all in the same year.

lumie: we had a house in manila. tatay bought land in mindoro, his family homestead. he entrusted the land to his cousin and abandoned it. the distillery too, he entrusted it to norma morales' family and it went downhill. he also started a casino, entrusted it to someone else, and it busted. he wasn't there to take care of things! so with all his constant moving around his opportunities went south. we didn't have any money. he lost all his properties and money by the time we went to college.

gloria: it's okay, we survived. "rolling stone gathers no moss." right? is that how they say it?

charing: *o sige siren*

agayla bii ya

what are your intentions with your questions

with your fishing, bari bari, asking permission

to pass through our lives, you apologize

and offer to omit or change our names

or poetize us into bite-size pulutan, easy to digest

wrapped in what, lumpia wrapper, salonpas, bandaid

to help us heal, from what, these difficult questions

yet you will bonsai trim, you will rotate the suckling pig

for slow hours and then pluck off the hot, crispy skin

so delicious, a bit of guilty pleasure, delicious

violence, oh don't be so dramatic, it's our culture

you don't need to be so careful with us, don't shrink

or make us shiny, sure we will be lying a little bit when we

laugh and say go ahead, we don't care, we're already old

are you trying to heal us or hurt us, is this a trap, ha ha

i'm joking, sure, you can write it just don't get mad if

i ask you not to write that part no not that part *agayla bii ya*

time of war

War is a woman's body.
We watch the house wrap itself around her.

~ maria bolaños, *sana*

japanese occupation (1944)
urdaneta, pangasinan

- - - - - - mom voices memories - - - - -

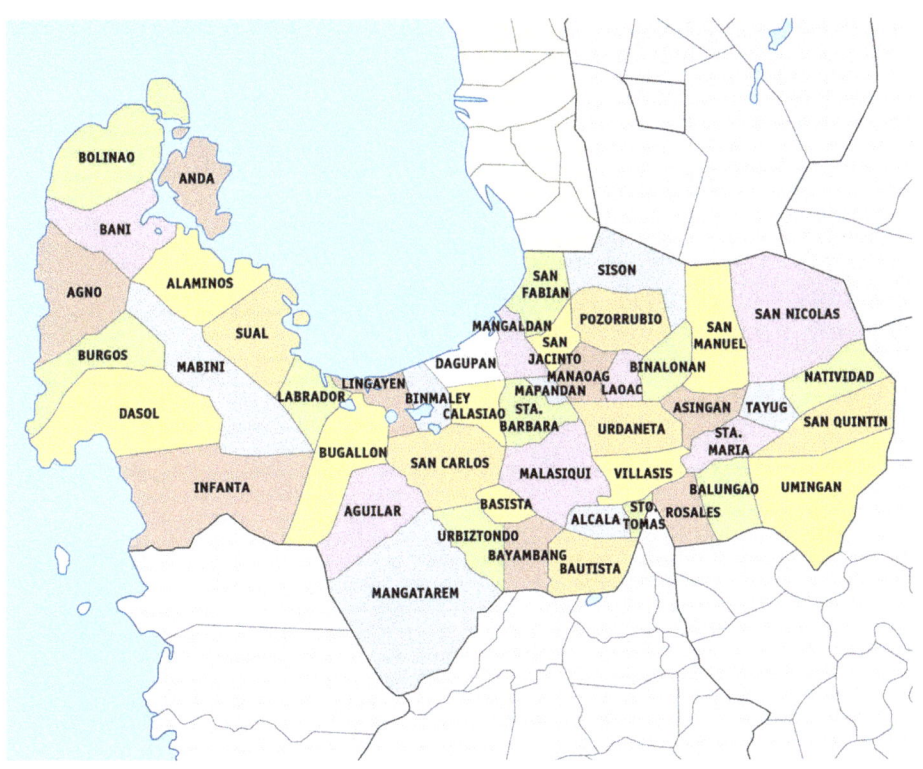

fire ants

one morning your aunty charing
and i are walking on the road
when we hear the planes coming

       bakalen   attack

we quickly lay down flat
on our backs in a small ditch

waiting. listening. tatay always
reminds us to keep still

suddenly the brilliant burn
the red fire ants are biting us

          rage   sanok

all over our sweaty legs, arms, faces
i think we accidentally disturbed their nest
with our bodies' surprise attack

        bales   revenge

i hope someday i can forget
the planes' sickening drone
warning us of invasion
reminding us to keep quiet

         suffer   irap

while the fire ants arrive in droves
feasting on our skin, the barbed mouth
bites then arched backs shooting
poison into us while we bite our lips
to stay quiet and we can taste
our own blood

        damage   deral

when the japanese soldiers arrive

they take over our housing compound
and the elementary school next door
to use as their garrison

        marutak   corrupt
        marutak   dirty

we hide in the banana grove
and watch the tanks encroach

caterpillar tracks crush our vegetables
steel teeth shred our orchid fields

        damage   deral

they idle in our gardens of sampaguita
diesel fumes choke out delicate blooms

        suffer   irap, manirap

before they spot us, we tread softly
until we reach the road, exhale
and race each other down to the river

to hide from the soldiers at night

tatay and the men dig pit houses
on the banks of the angalakan river

each depression deep enough to hold
a family of eight to ten people

ladders of bamboo lashed with twine
we grasp firmly while the elders climb

the men reinforce the earthen shelters
with bamboo framing and rooftops

so we don't get buried alive
while we are sleeping.

we are still allowed to go to school
and the adults do what they need

we listen for things to get worse:
rumble of tanks growing louder

or the day tatay tells us we have
to stay in the shelter all day, at least

until tomorrow, or maybe tomorrow
night, at least until all of this is over

kabaley   family

      depart   tayan, ontayan

            mampapasnok   angry

                  steal   takew, matakew

sari sari

our family store was on our land
on the side of the road near our house

the soldiers took whatever they wanted
without paying. but they were mostly young

and joked around with us kids all the time.
we were still just kids to them, thank god.

our neighbor anna worked at our store.
she looked japanese, delicate. alluring.

she was in her early twenties. she loved
to dance, and always let us sneak candy

there was one soldier who was very sweet
he came to the store each day to see her

he protected us girls from the aggressive
ones. anyway, he fell in love with her

later, the soldiers were ordered to evacuate
but he went into hiding. anna vanished, too

      yaamot   secret

          heart   puso

             marekep   beautiful

being exposed

strip   gisgisen, sigsigen

every night just before 6pm, the japanese
soldiers march down our street
and strip their clothes until they
are naked. they shower in the public
fountain. the one source of water
for the neighborhood.

dirty   marutak

i am ten, your aunty lumie is nine.
we fetch water for our family.
tatay makes us dress like boys,
we put on our brothers' clothes
tuck our long hair up under caps.

lakseb   naked

i don't know if the soldiers know
we aren't boys, but they ignore us.
sometimes one of them
lifts our water pails for us
when we struggle to hold them
up. our arms shaking while we
carry the heavy pails away

baing   shame

before, there are a few of them
that are very nice. they are really
cordial with nanay and tatay.
but then they start losing.

american soldiers

one of our neighbors gets romantic
with a black guy who is a g.i.

the teenage girls, we call them the dalagas,
do laundry for the americans.

one afternoon at the river, your aunty betty and i
are picking up what we think are balloons.
we have no idea that what we are collecting
are used condoms from the night before.

the g.i.'s sleep naked. we spied them
along the river one morning.

we play hopscotch and watch the planes
coming closer. we wave at them.

marutak	dirty		
marutak	corrupt		
sin		kasalanan	
	fear		takot

sisters
part two

auntie charing says

all ten of my births were easy.

they said i'm like a chicken laying eggs (cackling laughter from her sisters at the table)

after fifteen minutes, i'm done. no epidural or things like that.

all at home except for one time only with philip, i had to go hospital because they thought

it was twins. he was eight pounds when he was born. *matabataba*

mom says:

everyone went to a fiesta in calasio and left me home with your aunty char who was due anytime to have her seventh child.

while they were all gone, char said she was going to have the baby now. i screamed, *please don't!*

i found a big stick and threw it out the window to the neighbor's house to try and get help.

i panicked. i had no idea what to do. your aunty had to call her own nurse, get her own water, everything. she even boiled the water herself.

the nurse arrived, barking at me to go get towels. i didn't even know where they were kept!

when the baby came out, i heard it and thought it sounded just like a cat.

the next day, your aunty char was up and about, cooking rice. so. anyway.

i have the receipts, mom says

the sisters try to correct
one other on what
each believed
went down

voices grow louder
each one insisting
she remembers
exactly
what happened

i don't want
to interrupt them
but
damn

an elopement
a baby

no! she didn't
have the baby
at home.
yes, i know that!
i'm talking about
that night when
the dressmaker
mayor
justice
of the peace
the priest
all came to talk
to tatay
trying to convince
him to approve
of that guy

nevermind
ang sakit
na ulo
agi katawan

so anyway

auntie lumie says

oh, i have a book of stories for you, kiddo. your mom was already gone, she doesn't know. it was hell.

we had a house in manila. tatay bought land in mindoro due to the family homestead. he entrusted the land to his cousin and abandoned it. the distillery too. anyway, there's so much to tell you. he really was strict on all of us. but always worse for the boys. we were always with sinting, he told her never let us out of her sight.

one time i ran away to pampanga, it's near clark airforce base, because tatay didn't want me to marry this guy i fell in love with. he threatened me. (need story).

who was the guy? how did you meet him? why didn't tatay like him?

i would probably be dead if your mom and dad didn't petition for me to come over as soon as possible. tatay was looking for me everywhere, asking everyone if they saw me. it was 1966 when i arrived. my god, that was a crazy time.

we all lived together at borregas house. oh my god, you don't know how we were so exhausted all the time! i would take care of you all day, and then when i had to go to work, i'd strap you in the car and bring you to fairchild parking lot. your mom was just off from her dayshift and would meet us so i could transfer you to her comadre's car (you know, since your mom didn't drive.) then her comadre would drive you both home. this was when your dad was working graveyard shift. jesus christ, we were like ships passing in the night!

but we had a lot of fun. we used to drive to sonoma on saturdays to get eggs at that farm, remember, atsi glo? your dad couldn't keep still, like me. he always wanted to go galavanting even when we didn't have money, we would load up the car and go to golden gate park, ocean beach, even yosemite one time. anywhere just to see.

so, i met your uncle chuck at fairchild semiconductor. it's a long story, but i was panicking because my visa was going to expire. i ended up giving him an ultimatum that i was going back to mapandan because someone else there wanted to marry me.

were you really going home? or waiting to see if he would call your bluff?

we were already dating for six months. i couldn't wait anymore because i thought i was going to be deported. your uncle chuck saw my luggage near the door. he asked me if he could use the phone. then he called his mom. after he hung up he said, let's go. he took me to the jewelry store to buy a ring.

- - - - - - - - - - - - - - insert story - - - - - - - - - - - - - - -
what you thought happened after you left mapandan

artwork by frances mendoza

naani   **later**

i ask: i guess these days it is a bit easier for us to talk about mental health. about depression and anxiety. but i know this is nothing new, and i can imagine that you all just didn't talk about it, that you pretty much thought to keep any of those feelings to yourselves. did you ever feel depression?

i wanted to kill myself, the quiet one said. almost before i finished asking the question.
i have a book full of stories. we can talk alone another time.

the talkative one tells me away from the others, *my god, it was hell. I could tell you so many stories that you won't believe it. we can talk more later.*

**we don't talk about it being a problem
until it is**

                                    are you my family? my god?
                                        are you my priest?
                        if not, i can't talk about it with you

there is no direct translation for "mental health"

                you need anting-anting. did someone touch you
            on the shoulder when they passed next to you? when you
                visited home? maybe they put a curse to you.

                        you have to understand our culture.
                        our beliefs. you're not from there
                            so you won't understand.

or "mental illness" in the pangasinan language

                    the spirits might be angry with you.
            did you step on the small hill of dirt near the bugayong tree?
                maybe you disturbed the dwende. do you remember?

                            people will think bad about you.
                            they will say you are weak.
                            you are shaming your family.

nuances: it's more like sadness, stress, unstable.

better go visit the hilot, babaylan, albularyo, curandera.
they will instruct you exactly what to do. maybe healing oil,
orasyon while gliding an egg over your body.

better to just keep quiet. make your peace
with the lord. just pray. i will pray for you.
ask god for forgiveness. praise him.

ermen, deral, agmakayari,

and what you need to offer to ask forgiveness,
to remove that hex. hopefully it's not the red dwende
that cursed you. that's the most evil one.

so many others are suffering more than you.
it runs in our family. it's in our blood.
never mind. we just have to accept it.

tapis tapis san, atapis, ambagel

to want to be a saint

Magic mirror come and search my heart
Can you tell me what you see
There's a thousand voices whispering
Songs and you're the melody

~ Earth, Wind & Fire, "Imagination"

hay(na)ku: **to want to be a saint**

one.
mapandan, 1980
dear uncle joe,

my first trip
to the
philippines

i
stood in
front of the

burial
vault watching
your bones gently

pushed
aside to
make room for

tatay's body to
be slid
inside

next to you
you were
such

a small gray
pile of
bones

that told me
nothing about
you

- - - - - - - - - - - - - - insert story - - - - - - - - - - - - -
what you think pushed uncle joe over the precipice

two. sunnyvale, ca
december 3,
1997

       the phone call
       from my
       cousin

       uncle e shot
       two people
       dead

       then turned gun
       to shoot
       himself

       a festering grudge
       turned fatal
       fight

       with
       his housemates
       from the homeland,

       from
       mapandan to
       milpitas

       exploded on the
       eleven o'clock
       news

- - - - - - - - - - - - - insert story - - - - - - - - - - - -
what you think pushed uncle e over the precipice

three. nanay says
for two
nights

> *i never slept*
> *then last*
> *night*
>
> *i*
> *dreamed e*
> *came to me*
>
> *embracing*
> *me tight*
> *i said anak*
>
> *it's*
> *been too*
> *long*
>
> *since*
> *i've seen*
> *you, why did*
>
> *you stay away*
> *so long*
> *and*
>
> *then i realized*
> *he's only*
> *looking*
>
> *why*
> *are you*
> *being so quiet*

why are you
not saying
anything

then i woke
up. it's
already

five o'clock and
he is
already

dead
they bring
me here and

tell me he
is already
dead

four.
nanay turns
to uncle e's

    daughter
    now it
    is just you

    and your mom
    you are
    unlucky

- - - - - - - - - - - - - - insert story - - - - - - - - - - - - -
how you think you can wake men from nightmares

five.
uncle e
tried to settle

      the problems by
      signing the
      forms

      by getting anyone
      else to
      sign

      the forms with
      him, by
      leaving

six. a vigil
aunties on
sedatives

so much wailing
seeing their
brother

unable to open
his eyes
and

mom
swears she
sees the rosary

placed
so peacefully
in his hands

move
towards her
while she prays

seven.
the sky
is surreal today

      the coffin lowers
      the earth
      swirling

      clouds
      like avalanches
      in slow motion

      rain
      people careful
      about making sure

      the ones mourning
      aren't getting
      wet

eight. how long
do filipinas
mourn?

> when they heard
> the news
> each

> sister walked directly
> outside her
> house

> into the backyard
> auntie mer
> screaming

> auntie lumie jumping
> up and
> down

> mom standing still
> her body
> trembling

nine.
to want
to be a

      saint
      standing alone
      in the yard

      calling in the
      ones you
      love

We are in a spinning top
Where, tell me, will it stop?
And what am I to say?
Open our music book that only few can look
And I'll write a song for you, ooh-ooh

~ Earth, Wind & Fire, "I'll Write a Song For You"

brothers

1. i dream us, uncle e

fishing with my brothers and cousins
at coyote reservoir in 101 degrees

we pierce and thread restless nightcrawlers
wipe the blood and mud on our shorts

crack dumb jokes waiting for fish to bite,
practice roundhouse kicks like bruce lee

until *hey, i think i got something!* and
we reel in jackpots of smallmouth bass

until our kfc bucket holds just bones and ants
it's so hot we pour our cans of coke on our heads

the shade long gone from our side of the shore
where we squat and sweat, laugh hysterically

when you power lift a huge block of ice
slip and slide it over your belly to cool down

~~~~~~~~~~~~~~~~~~~~~~~~~~~

2. i remember

that early morning phone call
mom's *antoy agawa?* and sudden scream

being told you were dead, that you
had just killed two people, then yourself

my voice exploding in my head,
no, no, no, why did you do it, uncle, why

sound of gunshots glocked in my throat
as i sat numb on the living room floor

i never saw you angry. only joking around
taking us kids to mcdonalds after work

pretending you forgot your wallet
and then laughing at our shocked faces

your sisters said you were too quiet
when you were younger, as a teenager

how you wouldn't eat for weeks
and refused to leave your room.

your sister mer said she was so scared,
she would beg you to eat something,

beg tatay to just leave you alone.
said she knew all your secrets.

i wish i knew how to conjure you,
to walk beside you in redwoods,

huddled in fog, to dive into the sea
with you, surfacing only to breathe

i wish there were pills or potion
potent enough to shield us now

to sit with one another
eye to eye and in silence

without flinching or giggling
without small talk and lies

i would whisper *i see you, uncle*
it's okay. gala dia, come here

dear uncle joe,

will you tell me about the land?
how lush and colorful, how vibrant
because you nurtured it so tenderly
as if everything and anything at all
that you ever cared for in your lifetime
depended on how you kneaded
the soil with your hands

tell me how you swerved away
from tatay's fists, how once
when you were 16 he found you
at a bar drinking with your friends,
and made the police chief (his friend)
lock you up in jail for the night

tell me how you were 26 years old
and almost made it, how you were
next in line, the first one after mom
to leave for america, you already had
your papers and visa two weeks before
you took your life. where did you get a gun

i heard there was a vicious conversation
aunty charing yelling, tatay enraged
a torrent of accusations, who was to blame
for the bank foreclosing on the family land
that tatay worked so hard to keep, and
on which your life depended

to this day, your sisters argue over this land
should it be divided or sold, who is to blame
for years of misunderstanding and silence
they just want to hang on to tatay's legacy
they know your blood remains in the soil
they always say, it would be nice to keep
that land. our brother died there.

      nailiw ta ka   *i miss you*

uncle joe

uncle rafael says

i'm not sure exactly
>how old i was when kuya joe took his life. 17 or 18?
>i remember my brother was such a joker.

i wasn't home
>in mapandan when it happened.
>i was studying at st. louis university in baguio city.

i really don't know
>why he did it. i was completely shocked.
>suicide was more taboo in those days than now.

i wasn't home
>during elementary school years. i went to three
>different schools. it wasn't normal in those days.

i honestly don't remember
>much of my life with my siblings and nanay growing up.
>i moved with tatay to different towns where he taught.

i wasn't home
>i was told to become a priest and spent four years
>in seminary, only allowed to go home on christmas.

i really don't know
>exactly how my sisters helped me grow positively.
>my formative years were stormy.

i'm not sure exactly
>why kuya emy took his life. he was the quiet one.
>very protective. such a tragedy. incomprehensible.

i wasn't home
>in the bay area with the family when it happened.
>i had already moved to modesto with your aunty peggy.

i don't think it's easy
>to talk about mental illness, depression, anxiety.
>when i say *easier* i don't mean *easy*. absolutely not.

i really don't know
        why you ask if i have ever experienced depression.
        yes, of course. and i will continue to experience it.

i'm not sure exactly
        how we learn to accept so many things in life
        that we will never control. the inherent part of living.

i really don't know
        how to explain it but the only thing i'm sure about
        is that if we're alive we will experience pain, suffering.

i wasn't home
        i wanted to go to a place called nowhere, and do a lot
        of nothing with somebody named nobody. just for fun.

artwork by frances mendoza

descendants of angels

look. we are more than our scars. we hold the memory
of trauma in our roots. and still, here is a moment of pure joy.

~ Art 25: Art in the 25th Century,
Future Ancestors

cousin jennifer (naty's daughter)

in the philippines, no matter how pretty your name is
someone will always come up with a nickname for you.

my mom called me neth. short for jenneth.
my dad and oldest brother call me phey. no idea why.

i was born in barrio santa maria
mapandan, pangasinan, philippines

on june 20, 1969. i spent my childhood there.
when i was in first grade, dad would pick me up

after school and take me to dagupan city to eat
siopao and pancit, and we would bring some home

cars were only for rich people. i miss the freedom
of just walking everywhere: school, neighborhood

and during christmas time we walked to one house
and another and again until it was morning

no christmas shopping (again, just for rich people)
big family gatherings and caroling, some chocolates

i remember mom and dad struggled to make enough
money to pay for kuya joey's college tuition

for high school they sent him to mangaldan
he could attend for free if he played in marching band

i was lucky to have my high school tuition covered
with a scholarship for being one of the top ten students

i remember days we had no money to buy food
we just ate rice sprinkled with sugar or condensed milk

even before i finished high school i knew i couldn't go
to college. the money was already spent for kuya joey

i miss her every day. her smile, her giggle, her cooking
cassava cake, pancit, her delicious suman. her jokes!

i miss her calling me saying, "neth, come over
and get some diniguan" knowing it was forbidden

she was so strong, even when we had no money.
even when she found out dad was having an affair

just before leaving for the states. she still let him
come with all of us to start our new life here.

neither of us would talk much when something
was wrong. she would go for long walks to hide

her feelings. when i miscarried my first baby
i cried to her, wanted her to hug me so badly

but all she said was, "pray so you can pass this"
and then she got ready for work and left

i wonder if it was too much for her, a reminder
of when her own child, my only sister died

from measles when she was only three years old
we all got sick, but only she didn't make it

when we left for california i was barely 18
i was so excited to work and save for college

i heard there were tons of jobs if you aren't picky
i worked three: McDonald's, Taco Bell, and

a job in a manufacturing company. after a year
i quit fast food, started school during the day

and worked 12-hour shifts each night. exhausted
but needed to pay off our plane ticket debt, too.

i really miss my mom. good and bad days.
when she got sick. when i found out about dad

and that other woman. and that i had a half-sister.
i repeat the serenity prayer to calm my mind

i go for long walks like mom used to do, i walk
to our lady of peace and cry with mother mary

niece frances (naty's granddaughter)

my name is frances dela cruz mendoza
my main nickname is iska
from the ending of "francesca"

i was born in redwood city, california
on october 2, 2003
at a hospital that no longer exists.

i grew up in a multigeneration household
cousins, parents, aunts, uncles, grandparents
on san rafael street in sunnyvale, ca

my dad left home for america in 1987.
nanay arrived in 2002. they got married when
she arrived here, had me and my brother here.

a good memory? on halloween after trick or treating,
my brother, cousins and i sprawled out
on the carpeted floor of the garage to trade candies

dad would come home from work at midnight
and we'd still be there, he'd hang out with us,
laying on his stomach on the floor, too

grandma naty and grandpa onofre picked us up
from elementary school in the big '80's van and
babysat us while our parents were at work.

grandma naty took care of me when i was in
elementary school, she taught me how to watch over
my younger cousins, especially alana and jiela

she showed me how to handle a knife carefully,
her hand over mine, while i sliced two whole bananas
for their snack. once she showed them

how to make a simple paper fan, pleating the paper
back and forth. i was so jealous, i wanted to stay
home from school and make one, too

my sleep schedule? rocky. proper sleep or meals
almost nonexistent since graduating high school,
esp. now with my job, college, creating art, etc.

i rarely eat dinner with nanay and my brother
and dad works nights so our schedules clash.
sometimes it feels like nobody cares or notices.

when we visit nanay's hometown in the philippines
i feel totally cared for. my cousins or mamis
would always wake me for breakfast, *kain tayo*

when i'm there i feel i can relax with my family.
i sleep well, i eat well. nanay, ate alex and
my mamis make me feel safe there. protected.

i feel closer to nanay now than i did when i was
a rebellious teen doing a lot of things i should
never have been doing or experiencing

nanay never needed the american dream. she knew
she would be successful whether she was in america
or the philippines. it didn't matter. she is so smart.

i love how musically inclined she is. my favorite times
are when she plays her guitar in the living room,
sometimes i'll grab my ukulele and jam with her.

i struggled being open with nanay about mental health.
i carried not only the weight of my own emotions
and experiences, but also those of my friends

(trigger warning here onwards). i would stay up nights
in middle and high school, discord messaging
repeatedly to make sure certain friends stayed alive

and that i would see them at school the next morning.
i would give them my baon because they didn't have food
and often no money to buy food at school

i would date people to feel like i was in control
of something, to make me feel mature. i didn't tell nanay
about any of this, nothing about my mental or sexual health

because there was too much stigma to deal with.
for sure. anxiety, depression, definitely undiagnosed
ADHD + unmedicated.

it was worse in high school than now. i feel better off
now than five years ago. i have my support system
at work, school, and with my family and josh.

i always carry rocks, stones that ground me
when my anxiety gets bad. i think i sleep a lot now
to cope, too. it's very avoidant of me though.

avoiding eating, avoiding feeling, etc. I miss being
able to cope with everything just by creating art.
sometimes it's easier just to do nothing.

if i could change the way our family views mental
health, i would change how my dad acknowledges it.
which is to say not at all. i don't know

if he understands how his actions, his words
affected us growing up. i just wish our family
could learn how to curate a safe space for all of us

like learn how to apologize. i think so much of what
affects my mental health more than likely stems
from their own experiences and treatment growing up.

niece bea (charing's granddaughter)

my name is czarina fae angeles bongato
everyone calls me bea

i was born in mapandan, pangasinan, philippines
on december 12, 1990

i was four years old when we moved to california
i grew up in sunnyvale on johanna avenue

i remember when you and uncle carl brought
my sis inday and i camping for the first time

uncle carl took us on a trail hike and taught us
how to identify animals by the poop we saw

my first time snow sledding i flew so fast
and landed so deep uncle rey had to rescue me

when i was sixteen i went back to the philippines
to visit with nanay and inday. that first night

we couldn't sleep so we walked around for hours
there were barely any street lights

the sky was filled with so many bright stars
we just let the moon and stars guide us

even though i grew up with so many siblings
i always felt melancholy. it wasn't until later

when i was in the military and living on my own
that i realized i was suffering from depression

i was heavy into alcohol and drank myself numb
on most nights for a while. my friend helped me

get better and got me to a psychologist who gave
me my first steps to recovery. these days

i feel like me, nanay, and my sisters have changed
so much, especially after we lost ate bamba

to suicide. we were so heartbroken. so shocked.
grieving her did make us closer, we needed to be

with each other to cry and scream with,
to remind ourselves we were definitely not alone

in our sadness. in our rage. we love her so much.
we remember the ignorant uncles who thought they

were god, who stood without shame at her casket
and exclaimed *she will not get into heaven now*

i don't know if nanay will ever be healed. if any of us
will fully accept what happened. if we will be able

to call her name and listen for her to whisper back
hold space for each other even when you can't breathe

mamang charing? aside from having a big ol' booty
she was the first and only female butcher i've ever met

she was always cooking. the best empanadas, hands down
nanay definitely got her cooking skills from mamang

nanay? i love that she can admit her wrongs now
she's more patient, more accepting. she's changed a lot

when i was growing up, it was hard for her to admit
she was in the wrong for a lot of things said and done

how she grew up affected the way she raised us
i know she had it rough. habits die hard, nonetheless

and thankfully they can still die.

ascendance

We know there are no saints. At least this time, there
is no lowering into ground. I promise there is only ascendance.

~ Keana Aguila Labra, "All Souls' Day"

devotion

all of the years
of her life devoted
to his panic attacks
his emphysema and anxiety
trying to suffocate her

even when he got so terrified
he refused to bathe, got scared
when she approached his bed
with a wash cloth and bowl of water

when it finally happened
she didn't know

his oxygen mask had fallen off
in the middle of the night
she didn't hear him calling
for her, she didn't know

in the morning
she blamed herself
all of the years
in one scream

a good wife
novena
hail mary mother of god
pray for us

she did everything
she knew how to do

ate gigi,

you are the one i want
to interview most
but i've been so nervous

i'm no healer, no hilot
or albularyo who can cure
someone's infinite grief

who will it hurt, how could it help
anyone of our family, suffering
in their silence

i call you *the real daughter*
mom calls you hija,
speaking with you

there is an ease
she and i will never share
how do you feel as a daughter

as a sister, mother, lola
tell me about your kids
tell me about yourself

how you came here
what you love, what you can't stand
i want to know what you wish

i would ask, i want to know
what you don't want to answer,
what your silence will tell me,

it's none of your business
you will never understand
you didn't grow up there

tell me, *ask me something else,*
anything you want. i will write
what you have been wanting

to say, what you think
you want to say, in the name
of healing, of truth, of love

unable are the loved to die, for love is immortality.
~ emily dickinson

dear niece b,

when your mom called
and told how your daughter
was the one who found you
in the hotel bathroom

the belt around your neck,
our lungs collapsed
in grief, *why, why, why*
we asked over and over

again, how
could this have happened,
tell me it didn't
really happen

you were always so quiet,
why is it always the quiet ones
we have to watch
so carefully

i wish i could have pried open
your grief, released
a scream all of us
could have heard

you must have felt so lonely
surrounded by the loneliness
of other people,
why did we fail you,

why didn't we know
how to stop it, i'm so sorry
my love, our precious girl.
i'm sorry.

bamba

dear nephew,

we thought you had a heart attack
but you took your own life
we found the letter you left, asking
your kuya zaldy to take care of your son

     please accept me as you find me
          ermen   grief
            kabaley   family
                agmakayari   sick

i don't know how to honor you, little cousin.
i don't want to cause trauma. to trigger bad blood.
in my mind i am home, but i confess
i was getting drunk in the parking lot outside

     gathering is enough heartbreak
          journey   biyahe
            ambaingan   ashamed
               suffer   irap, manirap

while zaldy was screaming over your casket,
why did you say you're not loved?
don't you know i fuckin' love you, bro?
why did you think like that?

     what is missing: the verbs for healing
          abalong   lost
            yaamot   secret

and mom trying to calm him,
ok, anak. he hears you. he hears you.
and cousin rey trying to tell her,
it's ok, aunty. i got him. it's ok.

     what is lost: a little brother, son, father,
          blood   dala
            sorrow   ermen

jr

"Every chapter has to include an unexpected joy or tragedy, no matter how seemingly insignificant. These twists keep the reader's interest piqued, and from bogging down the narrative.

It is important to state here that it is almost mandatory for a successful narrative oral history to have two authors. Two sets of eyes are needed to catch each other's mistakes and to inspire one another to go beyond what they think they are capable of."

"Every ███████████████ unexpected joy or
tragedy, ██████████████████████████
twists keep the reader█ ██████████from
bogging down █████
It is important █████ ██████almost mandatory
for █████ history to have two
authors. Two sets of eyes ██████to catch ███
████ mistakes ██████ inspire one another to go
beyond ████████████████████

every unexpected joy
or tragedy
twists

keep the reader
from bogging
down

it is important
almost mandatory
for

history to have
two authors
two

sets of eyes
to catch
mistakes

inspire one another
to go
beyond

the bending of waves

When I was just a little girl, I asked my mother, what will I be?
Will I be pretty? Will I be rich? Here's what she said to me
Que sera sera, whatever will be, will be
The future's not ours to see, que sera sera

~ "Que Sera Sera", sung by Doris Day
written by Jay Livingston & Ray Evans

artwork by frances mendoza

hay(na)ku   maria gloria (mom)

november 14, 2023, 11am at home in the kitchen

we never talked
about those
things

mental health, anxiety,
depression or
suicide

never got any
kind of
sex

education or things
like that
never

when i married
i didn't
know

what i was
supposed to
do

tatay would go
through our
notebooks

and school bags
to catch
if

we were hiding
any love
letters

we never talked
so anyway
secrets

so anyway, i begin . . .

twenty-four years ago
i was slammed
with my first bout
of depression.

i had no idea what the fuck
was happening to me,
my body emptied
of feeling,

grounding and peace.
suddenly disabled
of sleep and the ability
to find my spirit.

i couldn't breastfeed kai
anymore, thought the pills
i swallowed to stay sane
would poison him for life

> *where is my mind*
> *where is my mind*
> *where is my mind*

- - - - - - - - - - - - - insert story - - - - - - - - - - - - -
how you fought against grief until you were numb

mom confesses

so, anyway . . .
i never liked durian. all my sisters did. i couldn't stand the smell.
i never liked green things. vegetables. fruits with skin, i always peel.
even grapes. tatay used to make me stay at the table until i ate everything.
i would wait until he wasn't looking and drop it under the table to the dogs.

you know i'm a scaredy cat. i don't like crowds. or places where people
are packed into tight spaces. I'd rather stay home. I'd rather organize things
around the house and in the backyard shed.

i just don't like people who talk too much, especially when they are just
tsimis or bragging all the time.

> masangi-sangi (literally, too 'mouthy', large-mouthed, or speaks in a very loud voice)
> matabil ang dila; mindlessly spills the beans (mindlessly reveals a secret to someone
> who is not supposed to know)

your dad took care of those things. i don't even know how to write a check.
debit card, you mean my visa? pin number? i don't know those things.
i told you, he did that.

medicare part a, medicare part b, medicare part d, medical, medicaid, opm, ssi
blue cross blue shield standard, blue cross blue shield basic, blue shield blue cross
whatever that stupid third cheapest level is called. ay agi! too much.

i'm scared of the ocean
scared of the wind
scared of being alone at night

i worry about you, carl, kai, josh, kiana, bill, jim, yuko, karen, britt, serena, blake,
your aunty mer, your cousin philip, your aunty lumie, your uncle raf. this tanga
trump. all these homeless people. all this killing. we can't even take care of our
poor people. this stupid country. atapis.

so. anyway.

anak na lassi

why do you keep telling me i'm stressed?
i'm not stressed, i'm just making a comment!
my god, i can't say anything to you without you
saying i'm stressed, i'm worried, stop worrying
susmaryosep. that's why sometimes i don't
want to ask you anything because you always
get mad. *anak na lassi.* just leave me alone.

mirror   salming

we both had boyfriends for seven years
beginning in our first years of high school
we broke their hearts. unintentionally.
tried to ease their pain. but.

our dads liked the ones we decided to marry
we each have two sons and one daughter.
all two to three years apart:

> james angeles biala: december 1960
> > william angeles biala: may 1963
> > > arlene angeles biala: june 1966

> carlen kai del rosario: april 2000
> > joshua kalani del rosario: november 2002
> > > kiana lin aiko del rosario: november 2004

boy,   boy,   girl
                    boy,   boy,   girl

you survived non-hodgkins lymphoma.
you survived breast cancer.

i feel almost certain in my gut
that i will battle cancer in my lifetime.

slow growing surface cracks in the mirroring:
i love to travel anywhere. alone or with others
you love to stay home. sort, categorize things
put them into boxes, label and place them
somewhere in the shed. just to forget where.
i go camping for a few days or on a short trip
and come back to dislocated toiletries
in my bathroom, can't find things i swore
were where they were when i left.

when insomnia and numbness found me
you had just started your chemo.
doctor said only three months
if you didn't begin your treatment
right away. so you did.

the night before i went into labor, carl and i were walking
at ellis school. i just want the baby to come now, i had said.

kai was born on april second. my labor was three hours.
you had fast labor with your births, too. in the genes?

you walked into my hospital room with dad.
i remember you trembling and starting to cry
as soon as you held your grandson in your arms

i remember pressing my face against your hair
whispering to you *see? your grandson is here.*
you'll be fine. don't worry

just before the memorial day weekend, i stopped sleeping
completely. i began to feel numb to everything. my body
no longer mine. i floated away beyond control.

the only time i felt i might be able to fall asleep was
when i was getting a massage. but by that time my mind
was swarming with whispering and humming that insisted
nope, you gotta do this and this and that and then this again
and i couldn't stop those voices. no choice or time to rest.

i didn't want to take pills. but i was desperate. zero sleep
and trying to care for my baby, breastfeeding, changing
diapers, breastfeeding, pumping, the house closing in for real

tried to keep a routine. pills weren't working yet
so i took ambien for a sleep that didn't feel like sleep at all.
fed kai, took ambien at 11pm to sleep, carl did night feedings.
i bolted awake after four hours feeling like i hadn't slept
for even one minute.

go for a run at 11am. the only time i felt a sliver of normalcy
was immediately after i stopped running. maybe ten minutes.
every agonizing day i felt i just had to hang on until after 3pm,
that if i could just make it past 3pm it would get better.
backyard windchimes clinking in the deafening silence
mocking me. i was suffocating in my own house.

where was everyone? the entire house and backyard felt
like death. sitting in the backyard swing. you would take turns
with kai. i felt so weak in my helplessness to take care of you,
to take care of myself.

i stopped breastfeeding kai. didn't want to poison him with my milk.

routine: make tea for you at 7pm. neither one of us getting sleep.
prednisone taking over your body and ability to sleep, exhausting you

the resilience of you. you were more worried about me losing my mind.
losing your hair. bandana wrap. sometime later, maybe between
your second and third round of chemo, we went to shop for a wig.
you looked like dora the explorer. cute, but. and didn't wear it too often.

i remember when you finished your six rounds of chemo. your hair began
to grow back, first a fuzz and then a bit longer, just enough for you to look
like a stunning buddhist monk. your eyes were alive. you were gorgeous.

we took a trip to hawaii to baptize kai and to celebrate your remission.
i took a picture of you holding kai on the beach. it was sunset and golden.
both of you shimmering with the sea. unbreakable. everything.

maria gloria angeles. mom

Let the moon with soft, gentle light me descry,
Let the dawn send forth its fleeting, brilliant light,
In murmurs grave allow the wind to sigh,

~ Jose Rizal, "Mi Ultimo Adios"

mom,

you always cry when you recite his poem
even now at 91, you stand in the living room
holding the broom like a microphone
and though we laugh it only takes a few verses
until your voice begins to quiver, eyes shimmer

he was our national hero! you tell us for the nth time
and remind us that you won first place for your recital
in high school. how you will never forget that moment.

> *don't pull weeds or sweep outside at dusk*
> *you might accidentally hurt the dwende,*
> *you can't see them when it's getting dark*

when kai, josh and kiana were little you always warned
them *don't go there, there's a mumu there*
when they kept playing in the backyard at dusk.

i remember you telling me years ago
i don't believe in witchcraft or those things.
why, you do? no, it's too much, i don't like it.

now you talk about the aswang that spooked you
in the front yard, its bright lights spiking skyward
from the grove of mango trees. you never told tatay
about it since he would just laugh and scold you, say
what a scaredy cat you were. your sisters knew
about the aswang but never told you.

nanay told you she used to see the kapre behind
the house, an unbelievably gangly man staring at her
and always offering her food. she repeatedly refused
and he finally left her alone. wistful.

they say that if you accept and eat their food,
he will take you away and you can never   return home.

talking about war

i tell mom that watching cnn coverage of the genocide in palestine
is to get the zionist pov. she snaps that she isn't really watching

just wants background noise in the room where dad used to watch
tennis for endless hours: billie jean, navratilova, and eckert to serena

to coco gauff. mom still sits in his old office chair with his fleece
sf giants blanket. sometimes when i check on her she is sleeping

slumped low in his chair, propaganda voices blaring while i watch
her eyes move swiftly beneath closed lids. maybe she's dreaming

of her daily argument with dad to *turn the volume down!* or asking
him to buy fish at spalding market. i imagine how badly she misses

arguing with him, telling him *shut up, honey. i'm trying to listen to the news.* while he says, *stupid news. it's all the same disaster.*

i wonder if the unfathomable grieving of a wife for her husband,
a mother for her child, of the last living person in a martyred family

will heal or destroy us. how do we play god. we've become too good
at blocking out the background noise. constant drone of whispers

confessing we don't know how to stop. slumping into oblivion
while malicious men draw maps, then rip and burn them for kindling.

mother daughter

mom   i have a long book to tell   you

     me   you should be writing too

         i   will

           me   you're 92

              maybe   you

                 should start   now

Sounds never dissipate
they only recreate
in another place.

~ Earth, Wind & Fire, "I'll Write a Song For You"

anting-anting

leave a blank last page for good luck.

everything is as it's supposed to be

at this moment

right on time

the sisters will scatter beyond

their sorrows

and ask us to recall them in joy.

in all the articulations

of *we did the best we could.*

panangasi'y diyos

dear readers,
a word

everything is exactly as it should be.

i remember a family member saying this to me when i was slammed
by depression for the first time. i had no words. completely shocked,
furious that they would say something so hurtful when i quite literally
felt like i was dying. because when you are *in it* you feel absolutely
alone.

i know they were trying to help. i understand the sentiment, the belief.
the universe will provide. all things through god. panangasi'y diyos. i do
believe the universe provides, but patience can be an elusive trickster.
and timing may not be everything, but it can definitely be an annoying
bitch.

i mean, you can't really say what's wrong? how come?

no. i couldn't. most of us can't tell you what or why. at least not when
we feel panicked, numb, or both. if you are lucky enough to not
struggle with mental illness, know that i would never wish it upon you.
when my mom was diagnosed with non-hodgkins lymphoma and told
she might have only three months to live, she still felt i was suffering
more.

at least i know what i have, she said. *and steps to take toward healing.*

depression is no stranger to our family, and likely not to any families if
we are being truthful. how do we recognize it. talk about it. ride with
it without stigmatization, shame. without silence. when we have been
told through generations that The Thing to Do is not bring shame to
your family, don't upset the flow. put it all in god's/gods' hands. pray the
rosary. pray for forgiveness but don't rock the boat. *this too shall pass.*

why did you write this book? the past is past, right?

when i started this journey i thought i could honor them by telling
their stories. that i could try to find some resolution for why two
out of three brothers, my uncles, took their own lives. how a niece
and nephew took their own lives. there is no clear answer. there is
unfathomable grief and anger. desperation, guilt, and avoidance. all
fueled by love with no marked escape route.

i don't know if this honors my family. the years of interviewing nanay,
my mom and her sisters, her remaining brother on earth, my cousins
and nieces, my ancestors visiting in dreams. listening and trying to
choreograph their stories through poetry. to serve as witness. so that
maybe, when our elder queens travel beyond to meet their beloved
sister natividad, and their brothers emmanuel and joseph, we can
show this book to our grandchildren. to their great grandchildren. and
hopefully the conversations will be easier, and happen more often.
maybe one of them will interview us, ask us what we know about
mental illness and patiently teach us the steps to take toward healing.

panangasi'y diyos.

Notes & Acknowledgements

Translation Index

The page numbers follow the print edition of A Thousand Voices Whispering. Words may appear multiple times throughout the book. Here we list their first appearance.

Because the author's family is from Pangasinan and speaks primarily in the Pangasinan language, we have denoted the language as Pangasinan. However, we understand words share meaning across the 177+ Philippine languages, and we acknowledge this kapamilya of Philippine languages even though we cannot name them all. All translations below are in Pangasinan, with many likely same or similar in Ilocano, Tagalog, and other languages or dialexts.

Additionally, in some poems, the grammar is not correct. This is intentional. This is the result of assimilation and the process of reclamation of a Filipinx in diaspora relearning their family languages.

12   **Bari bari:** A phrase used to respect and ask permission from spirits, especially when entering unfamiliar or potentially haunted places. It's a way of apologizing for disturbing them and asking them not to harm anyone.

12   **Mano po:** Bless me

14   **Lolo:** Grandfather

14   **Lola:** Grandmother

14   **Nanay:** Mother, or endearing term for grandmother.

14   **Tatay:** Father, or endearing term for grandfather.

16   **Tabi tabi po:** Similar to "bari bari" but in Tagalog.

16   **Dwende:** A mischievous spirit often depicted as a small, fairy-like creature. They are believed to dwell in nature, particularly in anthills, termite mounds, or the unvisited parts of houses.

19	**Tambal:** Remedy
19	**Bugayong:** A type of vine believed to have medicinal properties.
19	**Nanay:** Mother
20	**Akin:** Why
20	**Arawi:** Far away.
20	**Anak na lasi:** Originally from nakna'y lasi, hit by thunder, but evolved to literally mean child of thunder. Originally means hit by bad luck but has come to be used as a mild expletive.
20	**Sangi ka:** Open (command)
20	**Taynan:** To journey.
21	**Kapalaran:** Fate
21	**Bii:** Female
21	**Pikakasi, dasal:** Prayer
21	**Anak:** Child, son, daughter, endearing term for young person.
23	**Albularyo:** Folk healer, herbal doctor.
24	**Orasyon:** Recited or written prayers.
24	**Anting-anting:** A type of amulet or charm believed to provide protection or good luck.
24	**Hija:** Term of endearment for daughter, child.
24	**Engkantos:** General term for enchanted or magical beings, often with human-like appearance.
24	**Pero:** But, however.
24	**Panangasi'y diyos:** God-willing, if God wills it.
26	**Sige:** Go ahead, sure, okay. Also used to say goodbye.
26	**Gala dia:** Come here.
26	**Susmaryosep:** Jesus, Mary, Joseph! (expression)
26	**Ang sakit na ulo:** My head hurts.
31	**Tsismis:** Gossip
35	**Tita:** Term of respect for a woman or chosen identity who is slightly older than oneself.
35	**Kuya:** Elder brother, term of respect for a man or chosen identity who is slightly older than oneself.
35	**Enamorada:** Crush, infatuated with someone.
36	**Atsi:** Term of respect for elder sister.

39	**Antoy gagawan:** What happened?
40	**O sige siren:** Ok, see you later.
41	**Agayla bii ya:** Ah, this girl! (expressing exasperation. could be endearing or not.)
44	**Bakalen:** Attack
44	**Sanok:** Rage
44	**Bales:** Revenge
44	**Deral:** Damage
45	**Marutak:** Corrupt, dirty
45	**Irap, manirap:** Suffer
46	**Kabaley:** Family
46	**Tayan, ontayan:** Depart
46	**Mampapasnok:** Angry
46	**Takew, matakew:** Steal
47	**Sari sari:** Descriptive term for small, local store.
47	**Yaamot:** Secret
47	**Puso:** Heart
47	**Marekep:** Beautiful
48	**Gisgisen, sigsigen:** Strip
48	**Lakseb:** Naked
48	**Baing:** Shame
49	**Dalagas:** Young women
49	**Kasalanan:** Sin
49	**Takot:** Fear
51	**Matabataba:** Fat
52	**Agi katawan:** Expression of exasperation.
57	**Naani:** Later
59	**Hilot:** A practitioner of hilot, a traditional healing art form that uses massage and manipulation of the body.
59	**Babaylan:** A Filipino shaman, often a female, who acts as a ritual specialist and intermediary between the spiritual and material worlds.
59	**Curandera:** A female traditional healer.
59	**Ermen:** Sad

59   **Agmakayari:** Sick

59   **Tapis tapis san:** Unstable, borderling

59   **Atapis:** somewhat crazy

59   **Ambagel:** mentally ill

62   **Hay(na)ku:** A three-line poem with one word in the first line, two words in the second, and three in the third. Lines can also be 3-2-1 (reverse). It was created by Eileen Tabios, a Filipina writer and poet.

80   **Nailiw ta ka:** I miss you

86   **Siopao:** Steamed buns

86   **Pancit:** Rice noodle dish

87   **Suman:** Filipino dessert of sticky sweet rice in banana or palm leaves.

87   **Diniguan:** A type of Filipino stew.

90   **Kain tayo:** Let's eat.

91   **Baon:** Food (or sometimes money) taken to school, work, or for travel; for example, a packed lunch

102   **Biyahe:** Journey

102   **Ambaingan:** Ashamed

102   **Abalong:** Lost

102   **Dala:** blood

112   **Masangi-sangi:** literally, too 'mouthy', large-mouthed, or speaks in a very loud voice

112   **Matabil ang dila:** mindlessly spills the beans (mindlessly reveals a secret to someone

112   **Ay agi!:** Oh, my goodness! (expression)

112   **Tanga:** Fool

114   **Salming:** Mirror

118   **Mumu:** Playful term for monster

118   **Aswang:** A bracket term for shape-shifting creatures that have a variety of forms.

119   **Kapre:** A mythical Filipino creature also known as a "tree demon".

Partial List of Mental Health Resources for Filipino/a/x community

Please note: These are just a few of the resources available in the SF Bay Area and beyond. I am not endorsing any particular service or organization, so please contact them for all information. Thank you.

Therapinay.com
https://therapinay.com
Therapists and Healers who understand the Filipino/a/x experience.

One Down Media
https://onedown.media/read/mental-health-resources-for-filipinos
A non-exhaustive list of mental health resources for the Filipino community.

LEAD Filipino
https://leadfilipino.org/services-2/
LEAD Filipino provides a range of educational and technical assistance services, including supporting individuals and families with local referrals for behavioral healthcare and legal assistance in the San Jose/ South Bay Area

AACI (Asian Americans for Community Involvement)
https://aaci.org/behavioral-health/
AACI Behavioral Health offers linguistically and culturally sensitive services that help clients overcome barriers to care.

NAMI Santa Clara County (Crisis Support, Mental Health Help and Resources)
https://namisantaclara.org/resources-2/crisis-support-3/
For Mental Health Crisis Support, Dial 9-8-8 to talk, text or chat
https://namisantaclara.org/resources-2/welcome-package/
https://namisantaclara.org/resources-2/county-self-help-centers/

Filipino Mental Health Initiative of San Francisco
https://www.fmhi-sf.org/resource-guides.html
https://www.fmhi-sf.org/adua-network.html

Mabuhay Health Center
https://mabuhayhealthcenter.org/behavioral-health
The Mabuhay Health Center (MHC) is a University of California, San Francisco (UCSF) student-run free community health clinic targeting underserved Filipino-American residents of San Francisco's South of Market (SoMa) District.

Hilot with Verma
https://www.instagram.com/hilotwithverma/
Hilot is an ancient Filipino holistic practice dating back to pre-colonial times. The main purpose of Hilot is to restore harmony in the body, promoting physical, emotional and mental healing.

Hilot with Ilana at Malaya Botanicals
https://www.instagram.com/ilanaebrown/
https://www.instagram.com/malayabotanicals/
The style of Hilot used is called Ablon, taught by Virgil Mayor Apostol and carried through his family lineage. Ablon focuses on bone-setting, joint mobilization, and energetic flow — a practice of restoring harmony to body and spirit.

Highly recommended reading: Nervous: Essays on Heritage and Healing by Jen Soriano
https://www.jensoriano.net/books

> *i thank all nervous people who sense the dangers*
> *of the world and still choose love.*
> *i thank all children for giving us the chance to change.*
> *i thank water for showing us the way.*
>
> ~ Jen Soriano, *Nervous: Essays on Heritage and Healing*

Acknowledgements

I am deeply grateful for community that carries me.

For unconditional love and sustenance: my Angeles, Biala and Del Rosario families

To my Angeles family, whose stories are integral to this book, and especially to those who gifted me with precious interviews: mom Gloria Biala, Aunty Rosario "Charing" Bongato, Aunty Iluminada "Lumie" Steele, Aunty Mercedes "Merced" Pasag, Uncle Rafael Angeles, Ate Gigi Bongato, cousin Jennifer Mallari, niece Czarina "Bea" Bongato, niece Frances Mendoza. Aunty Beatriz "Betty" Ungos, Aunty Natividad "Naty" Mendoza (RIP), Nanay Benedicta "Bening" Angeles (RIP), Tatay Felipe "Eping" Angeles (RIP), Uncle Joseph "Joe" Angeles (RIP), Uncle Emmanuel "Emy" (RIP), niece May "Bamba" Costes (RIP), nephew Francisco "Jr" Ungos (RIP)

For bringing the poetry to life with music: Bill Biala, Blake Biala, Jimmy Biala, Yuko Tamura Biala, Masaru Koga

For evocative artwork on the cover and within the book, and for cover design: my fierce and fabulous niece Frances Mendoza

To the amazing Sampaguita Press pamilya (Keana Aguila Labra, Maria Bolaños, Kelly Ritter, Eric Asuncion, David Anderson, and all.) Your commitment to publishing black, indigenous, and POC artists; your belief in racial equity and social justice; your unwavering support for indigenous groups worldwide; and your clear opposition to genocide, white supremacy and colonialism are everything I could ever ask for from a publisher! The dream is real.

To new SamPress friends, including fellow authors and pamilya: Ellie Lopez, David Maduli, Kyle Doria, Shaena Mae, Reggie Imbat, Eric Asuncion, and Keana's sweet Lola Josie

To Keana Aguila Labra, who, to quote Genny Lim, is "dynamite disguised as sampaguita!" Your leadership, hustle, talent, and energy fuel us all. Ading, you radiate kapwa.

To the force that is Maria Bolaños. Articulate, compassionate being. #MVP editor. The meticulous care you took with editing and guidance while your life has been LIFING. Kindred one. Our book anaks growing together! Maraming, maraming salamat.

To Lorenz Mazon Dumuk. AKA Pogi P. My ading, my little brother with the biggest heart.

To stellar, kindred writers who graciously provided blurbs: Genny Lim, Juan Felipe Herrera, Tshaka Campbell, Yosimar Reyes, Lorenz Mazon Dumuk, Elsa Valmidiano, and Janice Lobo Sapigao

To Angel Dominguez, Lehua M. Taitano and art25: Art in the 25th Century, Maria Bolaños, Keana Aguila Labra, and Jen Soriano for kindly allowing me to include their inspiring verses as epigraphs.

To Eileen R. Tabios, creator of the poetic form hay(na)ku and OG pinay writer. Sometimes the only way through appeared to be hay(na)ku!

To the Montalvo Arts and Lucas Artists Residency Program pamilya: Kelly Sicat, Judy Dennis, Emily Borchers, Olivia Esparza, Patrick Ip and Jose Ortiz, the deep energia of studio 40 and fellow artists, deer, lizards, turkeys, red Flame Skimmer dragonflies, medicine walk forest bathing loops offered from ancestral unceded lands of the Muwekma Ohlone and Tamien people.

For creative inspiration, solidarity, "parking lot" energy, support and friendship: Quynh-Mai Nguyen, Robertino Ragasa, Vanessa "Pfox" Palafox, ASHA, Suzy Huerta, Tony Santa Ana, Frances Mendoza, Josh Domingo, Jayann Bella, Tshaka Campbell, Mighty Mike McGee, Scorpiana Xlynn, David Perez, Rob Pesich, Danny Thien Le, Gary Singh, Abraham "Abe" Menor, Tasi Alabastro, Chris Locsin, Jeffrey Lo, Miki Hirabayashi, Leianne Lamb, Karen Altree Piemme, PJ Hirabayashi, Pilar Aguëro-Esparza, Tamara Mozahuani Alvarado, Demone Carter, Joseph Jason Santiago LaCour, Rica Smith, Lehua M. Taitano, Nancy Hom, Avotcja Jiltonilro, Tongo Eisen Martin, Josiah Luis Alderete, Francis Wong, pc muñoz, Manikrudo squad (Tim Z. Hernandez, Paul S. Flores, Darren J. de Leon, Norman Zelaya)

For fierce Pinay writers, for all the ways you continue to fuel me: Jen Soriano, Janice Lobo Sapigao, Maria Bolaños, Keana Aguila Labra, Beverly Parayno, Michelle Peñaloza, Barbara Jane Reyes, Veronica Montes, Sasha Pimentel, Rachelle Cruz, Aileen Cassinetto, Aimee Suzara, Elsa Valmidiano, Eileen R. Tabios, Janine Joseph, Grace Talusan, M. Evelina Galang, Marianne Villanueva, Shirley Ancheta, Virginia Cerenio, Dr. Dawn Bohulano Mabalon (RIP)

To my mentors, my guiding beloveds since college days: Juan Felipe Hererra, Margarita Luna Robles, Genny Lim, Virginia de Araujo (RIP)

For bringing us together in creative, cathartic and community spaces: Poetry Center San Jose, MACLA, Contemporary Asian Theatre Scene (CATS), MALI, Art Builds Community, Montalvo Arts Center, Works San Jose, Chinese Performing Arts of America, Chopsticks Alley Art, Bloco do Sol, Art Boutiki, San Jose Jazz, San Jose Taiko, Japantown San Jose, Medicine for Nightmares, SF Flor y Canto, Asian American Women Artists Association (AAWAA), Asian Improv Arts, API Cultural Center, Kearny Street Workshop, FANHS-SCV, LEAD Filipino, YBCA, Philippine American Writers and Artists (PAWA) and forever and a day . . .

For my life squad: Kerr, Domingue and McCullough families.

For love and friendship: my bestie Rose Kerr from middle school and
beyond, sis Sheryl Domingue and the extended (and extensive!) Simon
family; Heather, Sam, Maddie, Michelle, Ryan, and Hannah (RIP)
Rickerl; Tina Iv, Nelly Torres, Anna Rodriguez, Jane and Trang Nguyen.

For my daily medicine: Stevens Creek Reservoir, Fremont Older Open
Space, Pacifica and Santa Cruz, and the ancestors who stroll and swim
beside me.

For guardian angels: dad Hermie, pops Carlen, Virginia de Araujo, Pua,
Cody, Pepper, Buddy. Thank you, Dad, for visiting me every morning as
hummingbird hovering over the same purple flowering salvia branch
when I step outside on the back porch to brush my teeth and greet you.

For my loves, my babies: Kai, Josh, Kiana, Dozer, Boba, Chewy and
Mochi.

For my Carl: my ocean, earth, sky, heart. "*river, river carry me on / to
the place where i come from*"

May the Universe hold you all close.

About the author

Arlene Biala (she/her) is a Pinay poet and performance artist born in San Francisco, CA and raised in the South Bay. She has been participating in poetry performances and workshops in the Bay Area for over 30 years and was Poet Laureate of Santa Clara County for 2016 and 2017. She is the author of several collections of poetry: *bone*, *continental drift*, and *her beckoning hands*, which won the 2015 American Book Award. Her latest book, *one inch punch*, was published in 2019. She is a 2023-2025 Lucas Artists Fellow at Montalvo.

Arlene's poetry has been described as "grounded in ritual object and ritual practice, mantras that resonate within the body and plant the body firmly in the world. Her work responds to the call of ancestors and our own broken bodies, spirits, and the spaces we inhabit. Her poems are prayer flags offered to those whose stories have been silenced, hidden, and ignored. Arlene's work centers on stories of family, of generations who have left their native lands to live in diaspora, particularly those from the Philippines. She writes poetry to serve as witness, to create space for recognition and dialogue toward healing.

About the artist

Frances Mendoza (they/them) is a Filipina painter from Sunnyvale, CA. They are pursuing their Bachelor of Arts in Studio Practice/Preparation for Teaching and minoring in Asian American Studies at San Jose State University. They work mostly with watercolor and acrylic to create works exploring their intersecting experiences growing up as a first-generation Filipinx-American in the South Bay Area.

Land Acknowledgement

This book was written on the lands of the Ohlone Tamyen People. It was produced on the lands of the Ohlone People.

As settlers on Turtle Island, the staff at Sampaguita Press acknowledge we are on the stolen sacred lands of these Peoples. We remember their connection to these regions and give thanks for the opportunity to live, teach, and learn in their traditional homelands. May we create connections with them, and may we learn Indigenous protocols to become honorable stewards of the land.

We encourage you, Reader, to:

• Amplify the voices of Indigenous people leading grassroots change movements
• Donate your time and money to Indigenous-led organizations
• Politically support the Land Back Movement

In line with these encouragements, Sampaguita Press supports Indigenous art and donates a portion of Press funds raised to Indigenous-led organizations.

In reflecting on our own lives and remembering our family histories, we must remember the legacies of colonialism that we have benefitted from and continue to benefit from as settler-colonialists.

From Palestine to the Philippines, none of us are free until all of us are free.

About the Press

Sampaguita Press is an independent micropress publishing house based in San Jose, California. We publish works by and for Black, Indigenous, and POC artists. We acknowledge the intersections of identity and support the LGBTQIA+ folk/x in the Black, Indigenous, and POC communities as well.

Sampaguita Press was founded in 2021 by poets and creatives who wanted to create a space and platform for ourselves, our peers, and other fellow voices who are underrepresented in mainstream publishing.

We strive to inspire progressive change. We acknowledge that change is made with solidarity. We honor and nurture the relationships between our fellow communities. We especially seek works that broaden perspectives and foster understanding.

We believe in racial and social equity. We acknowledge that Western literature and publishing are still overwhelmingly white spaces, and we are committed to amplifying underrepresented voices by providing attention and care to artists who may not have access to traditional publishing spaces.

We are an intersectionally feminist & womanist, inclusive press. We prioritize Black, Indigenous, and POC artists of all genders. We discourage hegemonic narratives; hierarchical structures; and supremacist, assimilationist, and normative messaging.

We are a safe literary & linguistic space, and we welcome chapbook submissions in non-English languages.

We support Indigenous rights and sovereignty over the land known as the United States. Our support goes out to the Indigenous groups everywhere in the world who have been harmed, silenced, and displaced. We encourage our readers to learn about and support Indigenous Peoples.

www.ingramcontent.com/pod-product-compliance
Lightning Source LLC
Chambersburg PA
CBHW051317120626
46547CB00015B/2281

9 781965 439104